In Full Flower

Gemma + Andrew Ingalls

In Full Flower

INSPIRED DESIGNS BY FLORAL'S NEW CREATIVES

RIZZOLI
NEW YORK

New York · Paris · London · Milan

First published in the United States of America
in 2017 by Rizzoli International Publications, Inc.
300 Park Avenue South, New York, NY 10010
www.rizzoliusa.com

Design: Su Barber

Rizzoli Editor: Julie Schumacher Grubbs

The front cover arrangement is by Studio Mondine.
The back cover arrangement is by Max Gill.

The images on pages 22–25 were shot on location at Rivertown Lodge in Hudson, NY. The images on pages 52–59 were shot on location at Spring Studios in New York, NY. The image on page 70 was shot on location at the Michael Ingram Jones residence in San Francisco, CA.

2018 2019 2020 / 10 9 8 7 6 5 4

Distributed in the U.S. trade by Random House, NY

Printed in China

ISBN: 9780847858699

Library of Congress Control Number: 2016954439

Preface

GEMMA HART INGALLS

The work of photographers Gemma and Andrew Ingalls has been featured in such magazines as Travel & Leisure, New York Magazine *and* Martha Stewart Living. *They live in Los Angeles with their two children.*

"Do what you please, follow your own star; be original if you want to be and don't if you don't want to be. Just be natural and light-hearted and pretty and simple and overflowing and general and baroque and bare and austere and stylized and wild and daring and conservative, and learn and learn and learn. Open your mind to every form of beauty."
— Constance Spry

Plants and flowers were life essentials for me and my husband, Andy, raised in Vermont and Northern California, respectively. My Vermont childhood offered up ancient lilac bush hideouts and harvests of chamomile flowers and wild blueberries in the fields; and when purple crocuses and yellow narcissus poked their heads up among the still snow-spotted April landscape, they symbolized a promise of warmer days ahead. In Andy's California, poppies streamed in colors past open car windows, ripe apricots and periwinkle nectar fortified, and handfuls of giant wild roses were picked and made into magic potions from inside the thorny forts of their branches. We found each other in New York, and, through photography, found our way back to the plants and gardens of our childhoods.

Over the years of shooting florals and gardens, much has been learned from the flowers, and the designers that work with them. We've discovered that little brings more joy than being on a flower farm in full bloom, or in a garage workshop overflowing with freshly cut blossoms, except perhaps to be able to see incredible pieces being built from the bounty.

So when our friend, Ken Miller, suggested the idea of making a book about contemporary floral designers, surprised that this particular book had not yet been made, we happily took the idea and began the work of making *In Full Flower.*

Again and again, we were spellbound, first by the sheer beauty of each stem and then by the process in which these twenty-one designers shape the flowers into fleeting pieces of art. Similar to a memorable meal meticulously created and presented, only to be consumed shortly thereafter, flower art is living, nebulous, timebased stuff, to be appreciated in the moment, and then it's fleetingly gone, back to the earth.

As we met each designer, we were amazed how small and closely connected to one another the group is, and how the ideas and styles of designing flow between them. Many of them have worked alongside one another as apprentices, mentors, or partners. Creative ideas are shared through social media channels, teaching workshops, and through collaborations—both at home and abroad—often using the same seasonal materials. More recently, sustainable flowers and seeds are shared through a slow-flower movement, an important effort started and maintained by a handful of the growers in this book.

We hope the following pages capture some of the energy and magic that flowers offer, and that the work inspires you, giving you a glimpse into the world and craft of this talented group of artists.

A collage by Alicia and Adam Rico, made from the remnants of an arrangement of peonies, garden roses, ranunculus, and hellebores.

Foreword

STELLA BUGBEE

Stella Bugbee is the editor of New York *magazine's style section* The Cut. *She has been a creative director and worked on many publishing projects in her career, including the original* Domino *magazine. She lives with her family in Brooklyn, New York.*

The glorious, ever-present floral arrangement at the center of my grandmother's dining table had a dark secret: it was at least 50 percent fake. Red silk masqueraders mingled with living roses, baby's breath, and plastic leaves; bright white carnations camouflaged pale pink imposters—a delicate deception. When admired, she often authoritatively proclaimed, "Elegant!"

The night before a party, the floral arrangement would become her obsession. She'd stand in a canvas apron by the sink, brandishing scissors, enlisting my help. I can still recall the feeling of digging my nails into the blocks she used to anchor the stems, the dense green foam crumbling between my fingers like freeze-dried moss. When we were done, she'd stand back, survey her work, and say with a wink, "Don't tell anybody my secrets."

She knew that flowers were powerful visual anchors of memories, that her guests would recall the food, the wine, the music, and the sprawling opulence of her centerpiece—a clash of pink against red against hunter green. Though the style of arranging was a reflection of the moment, her urge to create something memorable with flowers went beyond ambience or trend; she was looking for a signature style, a way of saying, "Remember me as I wish to be remembered."

"Signature" is a good way to understand the work of the floral artists in this book. Each draws from personal experience, global and historical influences, local flowers, and the cross-pollination of ideas found on the Internet, to create arrangements of singular vision. And those styles span the gamut from the simple glory of Ariella Chezar's three-dozen peonies in a single high vase, to Bloom and Plume's explosive, living sculptures. Moon Canyon's wild mix of tea roses and local grasses has a perfect, earthy glamour for the Los Angeles landscape, and Soil and Stem's whimsical installation of white blossoms in a barren tree remind us that flowers can alter our understanding of space and time.

Luckily, this book is not merely full of bold statements for bold occasions; there are dozens of examples of flowers here for every day. Studio Mondine manages to make just three peonies look lyrical in a tiny ceramic bowl. Studio Choo's imaginative reinvention of the wreath implores us not to settle for the boring old standbys. The less complicated pages prove that with a little study, we too can achieve a sense of our own style. Though the people in this book come from all over the United States, they have each added a vital new voice to the conversation on floral design—eclectic, curious, sustainable, and, best of all, both elegant and real.

FOLLOWING SPREAD: Cosmos and a Cafe au Lait dahlia grow in the flower fields at Ariella Chezar's Zonneveld Farm.

Ariella Chezar

COLUMBIA COUNTY, NEW YORK

Widely considered to be the pioneer of the wild, straight-from-the-garden aesthetic and the flower "fairy godmother" to many young designers, Ariella Chezar had a series of creative mentors of her own that led her down the floral path. "I grew up in a home where making a life through creativity was modeled for us by my mother, my father, and their friends," Ariella says. After dabbling in acting and studying classical voice, Ariella found herself in the studio of a family friend with a floral and garden design business. "She was surrounded by the most extraordinary assortment of flowers I had ever seen. The realization that flowers could be one's medium was startling, totally thrilling, and something I haven't tired of yet."

Ariella's trademark abundant style—loose, organic arrangements overflowing with the best of the season's flowers—has become *de rigueur* for a new generation of florists, and she remains excited about those who have embraced her more natural sensibility. "It's amazing to see how many people have taken up this work, running with it and interpreting it in their own unique way. At the end of the day, we're all just putting flowers in vases; there's not a heck of a lot of reinventing the wheel and yet everyone inevitably has their own palettes or gestures that define them, their own approach to making magic." Ariella travels the world teaching her particular brand of magic-making, and recently began farming her own responsibly grown flowers at Zonneveld Farm (her Dutch mother's maiden name, meaning "sunny field") in New York's Hudson Valley, hoping to decrease her dependence on imported materials and encourage others to do the same. The palpable joy she feels in the presence of flowers and through sharing flowers with others continues to inspire and sustain her decades-long floral practice: "The life force that radiates from a flower at its peak is literally breathtaking. After all these years, the magic and beauty of flowers still blows me away. The fact that I get to earn a living in proximity to them feels too good to be true."

A wild combination of homegrown and market-sourced flowers erupt out of a footed urn in the tumbling style pioneered by Ariella.

THIS SPREAD: "There is nothing more thrilling than growing and harvesting one's own flowers," says Ariella. FOLLOWING SPREAD: Freshly picked dahlias and zinnias from the fields at Zonneveld Farm, as well as greenery foraged from the surrounding landscape.

ABOVE: Peonies interspersed with garden roses.
OPPOSITE: An array of fragrant peony cultivars, all grown at Zonneveld Farm.

Max Gill

BERKELEY, CALIFORNIA

The flowers that adorn the wood-paneled dining room of Chez Panisse are one of the few worldly pleasures that can hold a candle to the delicacies that emerge from the kitchen of the groundbreaking Berkeley farm-to-table restaurant. The wild, rambling creations of Max Gill, the man behind the eatery's blooms for the past decade, are a perfectly organic fit with the restaurant's local and seasonal ethos. Long a passionate gardener, Max, who held various odd jobs while dabbling in the world of cut flowers in the form of creating arrangements for friends, says that his vision of the possibilities within floral design only expanded after he met Ariella Chezar. Working with Ariella as a mentor allowed him to develop his signature style—a self-described "classic Bay Area sensibility, botanically inspired with a focus on a flower's growth habits and natural laws."

Honoring the way that plants grow in the wild—and in his seven-thousand-square-foot backyard cutting garden—is key to Max's design philosophy. "I strive to find broader-reaching relationships between the elements I pair and to build a composition as if all the components are responding to the same light source." So, too, is his delight with his organic materials: "I've had intermittent affairs with a few different flowers—clematis, abutilon, but right now, I have a hellebore addiction; they're so modest, you have to lift their chins to see their exquisite patterns. And I'm generally lost if I don't get to play with vines of one kind or another!" Beyond simply the environmental benefits of using sustainable, lovingly sourced materials, Max takes great pleasure in doing so, just like his most famous client, Chez Panisse. "The plates speak to all of the senses. It isn't that a local and seasonal tomato is better for the planet, it's better all around! There is nothing like using materials that are at the absolute height of their development and beauty."

Lush layers of white anemone, citrus on the branch, and delicate vines.

"My garden offers an abundance of treasures; arranging flowers doesn't get any better than when you are doing it with product that you yourself grew," says Max. FOLLOWING SPREAD: Max re-creates a thicket of clematis with vines from his cutting garden in his potting shed.

FOLLOWING SPREAD: A striking combination of 'Bartzella' peonies, nasturtiums, and yellow raspberries from Max's cutting garden.

Alicia + Adam Rico

BOWS + ARROWS · DALLAS, TEXAS

Alicia and Adam Rico, the husband-and-wife team behind Bows and Arrows Flowers, draw on artistic backgrounds and an everything's-bigger-in-Texas attitude to create bright, bold arrangements out of their Dallas studio. Alicia, who started working in florals at a small shop in Brooklyn in 2007 while still a practicing painter, went solo with Adam in 2009 when the two returned to Texas to be closer to her family. Adam handles the larger installation work, while Alicia typically takes charge of the arranging, preferring to use fragrant, locally grown flowers like garden roses and sweet peas. She puts together her whimsical, gardenesque designs similarly to the way she applies paint to canvas: "I choose my color palette and build the arrangement using varying texture and form while keeping composition in mind."

The pair regularly takes on destination weddings, traveling frequently to Mexico and the Caribbean and occasionally farther afield to countries such as Thailand and Brazil. Alicia and Adam always incorporate locally foraged and farmed materials to create a sense of place through the event's tablescape. "Travel for me is a big inspiration. I continue to learn and evolve my aesthetic through experiencing new cultures and landscapes," Alicia says. "There are challenges, though—while foraging, we've crossed fire ants, tarantulas, poison ivy, and rattlesnakes!" A playful sensibility and a commitment to cooperation and experimentation run through all of the duo's local and far-flung projects. "Since we have full trust in each other, we can give honest critiques about how to make our work and ourselves better. Being married to your business partner and having two young kids can sometimes feel a bit crazy, but it also makes every day a new adventure."

A doorframe garland built by Adam and filled in by Alicia, with peonies, ranunculus, roses, and fritillarias.

The husband-and-wife duo at home: "We both feel so lucky to get to work together!"

"I absolutely love the variety and extremes that flowers take," Alicia says. "Arranging allows me to 'paint' with flowers by combining the different parts into a composition." FOLLOWING SPREAD: Alicia combines garden roses, amaryllises, ranunculus, and hellebores in her characteristically bright palette.

OPPOSITE: Alicia often turns fading arrangements into flower collages. Here, she's repurposed anemones, garden roses, ranunculus, astilbes, tuberoses, lilacs, nigellas, and tulips in a variety of neutral hues.

Erin Benzakein

FLORET FLOWERS · SKAGIT VALLEY, WASHINGTON

In 2001, Erin Benzakein moved her family from Seattle, where she had been working as a landscape designer, to Washington's Skagit Valley in search of a slower, simpler way of life. There, she set aside two rows in her new vegetable garden to spread the ashes of her great-grandmother and plant sweet peas in her memory, honoring the fragrant blooms that she and Erin would cut into bouquets during childhood summers spent at her home. After sharing the spoils of her bumper crop with her friends and family, news of Erin's green thumb quickly blossomed into filling orders for every single flower that she grew on her tiny two acres of land. With this first flush of sweet peas, her wildly influential farm and design studio, Floret Flowers, was born.

Rather than trying to compete with the massive commercial growers in the area, the family business remains small, focusing on producing high-quality, select heirloom varieties and specialty cut flowers. Floret's delicate, richly scented sweet peas, massive dahlias, and cheerful, tissue-paper-thin Icelandic poppies are coveted by other designers and are the building blocks of Erin's own textured, straight-from-the-field arrangements.

The considerable effort of running the farm is not without its rewards: "For me, it is so gratifying to grow from seed; there is this amazing amount of potential contained within each teeny-tiny seed, just waiting for the right conditions to burst with life." And by spreading the gospel of sustainable flower farming through her widely followed social media presence, Erin has cultivated a new crop of farmer-florists, all eager to try their hand at growing their own raw materials, often from Floret's own dahlia tubers and heirloom seeds. While she remains modest about the movement inspired by her own earthly endeavors, Erin never underestimates the capabilities of flowers: "I am constantly amazed at how they tap into our deepest emotions. They create joy, provide comfort, inspire happiness, and stir nostalgia. The healing that can come from the simple act of growing, sharing, or receiving flowers is really remarkable."

A rambling thicket of roses and bright peony bushes frame Erin as she surveys her flower fields.

Erin and Chris harvest 'Distant Drums' garden roses in the Floret fields. "My designs are a direct reflection of the seasons," Erin says. "Each bouquet captures a unique moment in time." **ABOVE, RIGHT:** 'Distant Drums' roses in one of Erin's signature abundant arrangements.

FOLLOWING SPREAD: Fresh-cut roses and peonies in Erin's studio.

Brittany Asch

BRRCH · BROOKLYN, NEW YORK

Five years ago, Brittany Asch of BRRCH never would have guessed that a career in the floral world was in the cards for her. Then a hostess at a Brooklyn restaurant, a curiosity about the weekly flowers on the bar led her to begin to create her own arrangements, a casual experimentation that allowed her to find what is now obviously her artistic calling. Brittany has quickly made a name for herself as a master of vibrant, otherworldly floralscapes for high-profile devotees in and around the New York City area, including supermodel Karlie Kloss and socialite Lauren Santo Domingo. A design course at the New York Botanical Garden, an internship at Saipua, and freelance gigs with established florists like Taylor Patterson and Sarah Winward all allowed her to hone her technique and her aesthetic, which today bears less resemblance to the trend of wild, straight-from-the-garden arrangements and more to a pop-driven, Technicolor palette of highly styled, layered blooms.

Brittany says that while her work has always been informed by different natural environments, "I no longer identify with the landscape in which I was raised, the Hudson Valley—lush, seasonal, viney, and swampy. Now, I create imaginary climates from worlds that do not exist." Swarms of tropical and exotic varieties—anthuriums, cascading orchids, proteas, spotted begonia leaves—punctuated by native, seasonal standbys—often garden roses, peonies, poppies—engender a floral fantasy, a symphony of bright pops of color and textures that is at once both deeply of the earth and consciously artificial. Brittany, who trained at Boston's Berklee School of Music as a singer and performer, seeks to tell stories through the floral medium, eliciting a heightened appreciation of the beauty of the natural world while drawing attention to the obviousness of the human hand in her creations. "I like to think that there is an element of fantasy in everything I make. One of the great joys I derive from my work is knowing that I'm giving people something that can't be in found in their backyards."

A unique combination of anthuriums, fuchsias, gloriosa lilies, banana flowers, and a poppy.

Brittany often incorporates tropical plants and flowers into her arrangements: "They're like a dose of Vitamin D in my work," she says.

OPPOSITE: An allium flower shoots out of an arrangement that includes locally foraged leaves as well as the spiky devil's thorn.

Brittany is known for juxtaposing traditional, seasonal flowers, like peonies and roses, with unexpected choices, like orchids, anthuriums, fuchsias, and begonia leaves.

Emily Thompson

EMILY THOMPSON FLOWERS · NEW YORK, NEW YORK

Tucked away in Manhattan's South Street Seaport is the flower studio of Emily Thompson Flowers, housed in a sunny building adorned with terracotta sea monsters and cast-iron starfish. The eccentric creatures that lie outside the workspace and boutique give those passing through the doorway a taste of what is to be found inside—a veritable cabinet of floral curiosities out of which some of the city's most magnificent, outrageous, modern designs emerge. Emily, who became widely known after being selected to do the White House's annual holiday floral installation in 2011, came to flowers organically. After receiving an MFA in sculpture from UCLA, she worked, by her own admission, as a "starving artist," assisting artists Vija Celmins and Roxy Paine, and in her own time crafting fine-art pieces that served as precursors to her botanical stylings—ceramic and wax sculptures and decorative objects. As she began taking on wedding floral design jobs for friends, she realized that she "had incredibly strong opinions about how the flowers should be, and eventually, all of the thought and technique I had put into sculpture migrated into this medium."

Anchored in a surrealist tradition and a self-proclaimed love for flowers with "teeth"—unusual blooms and organic materials that chafe against the traditional notion of beauty—Emily's aesthetic tends toward the wild, dramatic, and grand, often incorporating twisting stalks of allium, spiky carnivorous flowers, and thorny, gnarled branches alongside tiny, exquisite species of intricately patterned fritillarias or rare orchids. Her rigorous attention to the movement and gesture of these unique ingredients hints at her roots in sculpture. A passion for her raw material is first and foremost what drives her work: "I am immersed in this endless, infinite variety of nature's production, and can think of nothing greater to draw my imagination and my energies. The flowers are their own reward."

Emily's characteristic drama, whimsy, and attraction to the "weird and weedy" can be seen in her ongoing series of large-scale installation pieces for The Modern restaurant at the Museum of Modern Art. For those arrangements, she draws inspiration from the museum's abstract collections, the seasons, and the weather; to her delight, "the big pieces often look like a gale just blew inside." Emily confesses that while her spectacular creations and the sweeping narratives she builds into her work are in service to a client, they often serve to satisfy her own aesthetic fantasies. "But everything I do," she explains, "is to say, 'LOOK, LOOK! Look harder and sooner and longer!'"

Passionvine, smokebush, garlic scapes, and foraged branches spill artfully out of their vessel.

ABOVE, LEFT: A glasswing butterfly alights on a poppy. FOLLOWING SPREAD: Emily's background as a sculptor and her boundless imagination are evident in this installation featuring hornet nests, magnolia branches, poppies, and live butterflies.

"I want our flowers to always have character," Emily says. "Above all, my work should always, always be interesting." OPPOSITE: A signature wild and weedy creation comes alive at night in a greenhouse.

Amanda Luu + Ivanka Matsuba

STUDIO MONDINE · SAN FRANCISCO, CALIFORNIA

The kinetic energy of San Francisco's Mission District, brimming with artists, craftspeople, and tech start-ups, spills over into the tiny workspace of Studio Mondine, the floral partnership of Amanda Luu and Ivanka Matsuba. The pair found their way to the flower arts at different points in life—for Amanda, it was after being pulled away from a "left-brained data science career" by the creative allure of the San Francisco flower world; and for Ivanka, as a young girl in Slovakia making arrangements for family celebrations. The two met in 2013 while doing freelance floral gigs, bonding over a pared-down aesthetic and a whatever-it-takes work ethic. Appropriately enough, *mondine* originated in the nineteenth century to name the spirited, dedicated women who performed the challenging work of cultivating rice in Northern Italy. A motto of "simple but striking" anchors Amanda's and Ivanka's design ethos; flowers that feel effortless are carefully selected at the wholesale market, foraged from the side of the road and friends' backyards, or grown in the studio's cutting garden, then thoughtfully arranged: "We subscribe to the Japanese aesthetic of 'su,' meaning plain or unadorned, and we believe that simplicity can be more appealing than over-the-top luxury."

Amanda's and Ivanka's stunning arrangements—whether minimal and Ikebana-inspired or lush and overflowing—highlight each season's most special, unusual flowers. Spring, their favorite season, ushers in a palette of richly colored hellebores, blooming branches of quince, spirea, and dogwood, tree peonies, bearded irises, and the first flush of local heirloom roses. Though the two take inspiration from the surrounding artistic community and the Bay Area landscape, it is the blooms themselves—and their evanescence—that provide the richest material for the design duo. Says Amanda, "Flowers helped me shake loose the idea that only durable things were valuable. In a way, creating with a live medium has become a meditation on what remains when everything else fades away."

"In every floral work, we hope to capture a moment in time and place—however fleeting that may be," Amanda says.

OPPOSITE: A dogwood *kokedama*, or moss-wrapped soil ball, a Japanese variant of bonsai.

Whether they're creating spare, Ikebana-style work or more lush bouquets, Amanda and Ivanka consider the placement of each and every flower: "Our flowers are pared down, unadorned, but always intentional."

OPPOSITE: Delicate fallen petals become part of the arrangement.

Maurice Harris

BLOOM AND PLUME · LOS ANGELES, CALIFORNIA

Larger-than-life arrangements come easily to Maurice Harris, a Los Angeles florist whose work overflows with personality and vibrance. Based in Echo Park, Maurice got his start managing the visual display for Juicy Couture retail stores, first doing small arrangements for the office and then becoming the brand's in-house florist. Floral design was a logical transition from his previous work: "I've always been drawn to flowers for their ability to transform spaces and environments," says Maurice. He refers to his signature style as "natural opulence," seeking to craft dramatic, asymmetrical florals and installations that seamlessly bridge the organic and manmade worlds, such as a structural column covered with wild ferns or by "planting" thousands of stems of roses in the ground: "I love designs that are basically naturally impossible but that appear completely effortless."

Taking a cue from his background in fashion, Maurice considers color, texture, and pattern when plotting his lavish floral creations. In addition to the seasonal favorites—lilacs in the spring, eremuri and dahlias in summer, pear branches and blushing brides in fall—that provide the building blocks for his work, Maurice imbues all his designs with his comedic sensibility, naming each arrangement he posts on social media and crafting an individual narrative for each. A mix of greens, thistles, kumquats, and hellebores becomes Sister Green Goddess—"Sister Green knows how to stand out in the crowd while blending in beautifully with her surroundings." A sweeping combination of white peonies, ranunculus, and anemones is christened Madea P'Oneigh, who "keeps a clean house, a clean record, and even cleaner conscience." Maurice's wicked sense of humor and flair for the wild and whimsical mean that he occupies a unique niche in the Los Angeles floral community. Says Maurice, "For me, it's all about pushing the boundaries of traditional floral design and curating an unexpected experience."

Artichokes and a set of hands add a surprising touch to one of Maurice's floral creations.

Maurice's characteristic sense of drama and playfulness shine through in his vibrantly colored, U-shaped arrangements.

OPPOSITE AND FOLLOWING SPREAD: Human hands hold up Maurice's creations. ABOVE, RIGHT: Maurice works with peonies in his studio, the walls of which are adorned with his own photography-based floral projects.

Amy Merrick

BROOKLYN, NEW YORK

A self-proclaimed floral gypsy, Amy Merrick has spent the past several years traveling the world teaching flower workshops and searching for inspiration and beauty. Amy, who started her flower business in Brooklyn in 2011, rapidly became one of the most sought-after florists in New York City before deciding to indulge her wanderlust. Even with clients clamoring for her lush, free-flowing designs, Amy freely admits that leaving the city's crowded flower scene to traverse the globe was the best creative decision she's ever made: "I have a deeper respect for flowers—their power, purpose, and how they affect us. I care less about arrangements per se, and more about getting people to see nature in a more intimate way."

Today, Amy eschews creating flowers for high-end events in favor of sharing her craft with others, teaching workshops in Japan, France, and England. "I'm hoping to open people's eyes to the ridiculous beauty that we all pass every day. Showing people what I love about nature feels like a much more authentic expression of myself than making wedding flowers." The artfully messy arrangements that defined her style for so long—chock-full of the season's best blooms snagged from the New York City wholesale flower market—have evolved, too, largely as a result of Amy's extended study with Ikebana masters in Japan: "My work is becoming simpler and more humble in flower selection; I want people to feel the sunlight and a breeze blowing through my arrangements. I just want to be a magnifying glass to show people the beauty of flowers as they are."

No matter how far her travels take her, the coming of summer will always draw Amy back to her family's New Hampshire retreat, Elmwood, just in time to see her favorite flower—the heavenly scented lily of the valley—carpet the woods surrounding her home. A childhood spent running wild at Elmwood imbued Amy with a deep sense of family history, magic, and wonder at the natural world—qualities key to her ethereal floral designs. Says Amy, "I get giddy thinking about becoming an old woman and returning to Elmwood with a lifetime's worth of natural observations. How lucky am I as a florist to get to witness nature unfold and also be a part of it, too?"

Amy walks toward her New Hampshire summer home, Elmwood, which has been in her family since 1801.

Amy arranges wildflowers foraged from around her family's property.

Amy crafts miniature scenes from flowers and plants foraged from Elmwood's property. OPPOSITE: A wild blueberry branch that grows at the water's edge shades water lilies from the lake. ABOVE: Pink lady's slippers and ferns recreate the forest floor.

FOLLOWING SPREAD: Wildflowers flank their two-dimensional counterparts in the field drawing book of Amy's great-great-grandmother, a botany student at Wellesley College in the 1870s, who catalogued the very same varieties that still grow around the family's house today. "Elmwood instilled in me a profound respect for nature," Amy says.

Taylor Patterson

FOX FODDER FARM · BROOKLYN, NEW YORK

"I was always attracted to the idea of working with flowers," says Taylor Patterson of Brooklyn's Fox Fodder Farm. "Who isn't? But I thought it was something I would do when I was sixty-seven, not twenty-seven—it was a retirement plan of sorts." When the painter-turned-florist found herself at a crossroads after a summer gig working for a landscape designer, she took a position at a New York City flower shop where she learned the basics of floral design and the work ethic necessary for the job. Her own venture, Fox Fodder Farm—so named for her family's Delaware farm, quickly landed on the floral map after *Vogue* published the boho-chic flowers that she created for jewelry designer Pamela Love's Montauk wedding. Though her work today tends toward a significantly more structural, Ikebana-inspired aesthetic—large focal flowers like peonies and ranunculus, balanced with soft, weeping amaranthus and greens, and punctuated with surprising, bright tropical blooms—the wildness of her first major floral project continues to crop up in her designs: "There are times when all I want to do is create pieces that resemble messy wildflower fields and then times that I reject all of that and strive for a style that is modern and clean; days when I hate color and days when I surround myself with an oversaturated mix of palettes."

Taylor, who cites Dutch landscape designer Piet Oudolf as her primary inspiration—"I want my life to be a Piet Oudolf meadow garden"—brings the patrician sensibility of the rambling farm on which she grew up, as well as a painterly eye, to the arrangements she crafts for her wedding and weekly clients in New York City. "My paintings were always certain scenes in nature that embodied a sort of simple serenity. What I love about working with flowers is that while you can experiment with so many styles, I still find that at the end of the day it's the simplest things that speak to me—a single, perfect garden rose or a tangle of cosmos gets me every time."

Taylor at home at her family's Delaware property, Fox Fodder Farm, her floral business's namesake.

“There are times when I am inspired by the beauty of simplicity,” Taylor says. “Other times, though, it’s all about a gorgeously ornate composition and the challenge that comes with creating that.” **ABOVE:** Taylor takes an Ikebana-inspired approach to an iris arrangement.

Mandy + Steve O'Shea

MOONFLOWER · COMER, GEORGIA

Just outside of Athens, Georgia, lie five acres of farmland that serve as the life, work, heart, and soul of the dynamic husband-and-wife team, Mandy and Steve O'Shea. In 2011, after moving back to Georgia from California, where Mandy tended to a vegetable and cut-flower garden on an organic olive oil ranch and Steve worked with renewable fuels, the two bought the property that would become Three Porch Farm. Combining their talents to grow cut flowers and organic fruit on the entirely solar- and waste-vegetable-oil-powered farm, Mandy and Steve maintain a firm commitment to sustainability that extends to their floral design practice, Moonflower, for which they produce or forage all the materials that go into their arrangements: "Every element of our work is both informed by and derived from our immediate surroundings—nature is always our provider and our muse."

A subtropical growing climate means that the farm offers a bountiful harvest for much of the year; and each season brings a new cast of blossoms to star in Moonflower's wild and flowing designs—anemones, peonies, zinnias, cosmos, and dahlias take turns as the showstopping focal flowers. In addition to their carefully cultivated blooms and fruits, Mandy and Steve add to their arrangements unexpected touches collected from their property and the surrounding woods—seed pods, unique grasses, briars, and branches—seeking to mirror their environment for weddings and events: "Nature in the sultry south is rarely ever tight and contained and our job is to emulate its beauty. There's so much to be inspired by in our daily life—a walk through the fields or the woods, the architecture of an old building, or the art of friends and loved ones." The seed-to-vase nature of Mandy and Steve's operation makes for a deep, almost parental connection to their finished product as they tend to the flowers from germination to harvest to arranging and delivering. Says Steve, "After every event we always try to take a minute to look around at the newly flower-filled space. Those aren't just flowers sitting on the table—that's our life. It's beautiful and rewarding and makes us eager to keep growing and creating."

Branches and vines gathered from around Steve and Mandy's farm find a home among spring's brightest blooms.

"We love the opportunity to create with the beautiful flowers that we have put so much care into growing. The excitement begins when the seeds of our flowers first start to germinate—there is endless hope and possibility in a germinating flower," Steve says. FOLLOWING SPREAD: Poppies find a home in a wheat field at Three Porch Farm.

"Our flowers and our designs tell the story of the beauty of seasonality," Mandy says.

Sarah Ryhanen

SAIPUA · BROOKLYN, NEW YORK

The art of arranging comes naturally to the grande dame of the Brooklyn flower world, Sarah Ryhanen of Red Hook's Saipua, though her early design practice took on a slightly less glamorous form. "As a kid, I loved to arrange the knickknacks in my room—Absolut vodka ads, candlesticks, objects from the home goods aisle at T. J. Maxx. I like to decorate, though I've always carried a lot of guilt with regard to my seeking beauty just for beauty's sake." She found her true calling in flowers when her partner, Eric Famisan, gave her a bouquet of black dahlias for her twenty-fifth birthday. "I had never received anything so beautiful before and was hooked on flowers from there on, noticing how they made me feel and made my dumpy apartment feel really elevated and special." In 2006, Sarah elevated the art of arranging entirely when she and Eric opened Saipua. She specializes in the artfully imperfect, the wild, overflowing, and occasionally macabre. The self-proclaimed "closeted romantic" gravitates toward garden roses and whatever happens to be blooming on her upstate New York flower farm, World's End, in soft, moody colors: rose, mauve, brown, ink, amber. "My aesthetic is abundant, tumbly, sometimes sort of dead looking," Sarah says. "That's what I love the most—flowers on the verge."

Sarah takes palette inspiration from "roadside wildflowers, Benjamin Moore paint swatches, and the old shipping containers stacked up by the Saipua studio." Her obsession with color, in combination with the exquisite specialty flowers grown at World's End, imbues Sarah's work with a deep sense of her refined artistry and heady connection to the natural world: "The act of growing, cutting, and arranging with my own raw materials and the season in mind creates a subtle yet appreciable energy that is thick with my experiences and relationship to nature." Largely cited as being responsible for engendering the foraged, botanically driven trend of arranging, Sarah has fostered the talent of many prominent designers such as Amy Merrick and Brittany Asch, among others, through Saipua's internship program and the Little Flower School, which she runs with her friend Nicolette Owen. "The successes of my former students and interns inspire me and make me work harder; I always think a rising tide floats all boats. And more people paying attention to natural, seasonally inspired flowers is a world that I want to live in."

A sweeping composition of just-past-their-prime flowers and vines arches against a marble backdrop in Sarah's studio.

Sarah at work in her light-filled Brooklyn studio. "What's in peak season always jumps out at me," Sarah says. "Nature dictates the color palette and the raw materials—all my work is done for me!"

ABOVE: A hand-tied bouquet includes treasured cuts from Sarah's upstate New York farm, World's End—kousa dogwoods, martagon lilies, and foxgloves.

Nicolette Camille

NICOLETTE OWEN · BROOKLYN, NEW YORK

Growing up in her mother's and grandmother's gardens in New York's Hudson Valley impressed Brooklyn-based Nicolette Owen with a lifelong passion and appreciation for the natural world. "Perhaps the most important lesson I learned as a girl was that flowers and gardens were a special gift and that gift was meant to be shared," says Nicolette. While working as a photo editor at *Domino* magazine, Nicolette began creating flower arrangements for friends, family, and the occasional photo shoot for the magazine, turning her talent into a full-fledged business—Nicolette Camille—in 2008. Known for her graceful, hauntingly beautiful arrangements, Nicolette seeks to capture a quiet poetry with her work, preferring to work with flowers that have the most evanescent life spans—delicate garden roses, tree peonies, blossoms on the branch, and bearded irises. "Capturing these fleeting blooms at their peak is the ultimate way to honor their inherent beauty."

Nicolette's adoration for her medium is obvious in her exquisitely composed, painterly designs and masterful use of color, a byproduct of her background in fine arts. "Finding new ways to incorporate hues and shades is endlessly inspiring to me. It's always best to start off subtly and find the delicate relationship between colors and textures—sometimes as simple as the conversation between gloss and matte. There are infinite ways to look at and learn from color." The Little Flower School, cofounded in 2007 with Sarah Ryhanen of Saipua, represents another fruitful partnership for Nicolette, as the two have traveled the world teaching floral design. "It's been an incredible shared experience working with someone with whom I share so many aesthetic preferences, but with just enough difference to keep things exciting," Nicolette says. "It's truly a gift to have a creative partner that I can trust fully and wholly—a rare gem."

Nicolette captures the essence of spring with a striking mix of tulips, ranunculus, fritillaria, hellebore, poppies, and spirea.

Nicolette harvests fall foliage from the shared garden at her Brooklyn studio.

THIS SPREAD: Nicolette incorporates exquisite bearded irises from Oregon's Schreiner's Iris Gardens into her tumbling arrangements. "I adore flowers to the ultimate extent of the word," she says. "I marvel at nature's imperfect perfection."

FOLLOWING SPREAD: Bearded irises from Schreiner's Iris Gardens.

Jill Rizzo + Alethea Harampolis

STUDIO CHOO · SAN FRANCISCO, CALIFORNIA

The phrase "cookie cutter" is not easily—or ever—applied to San Francisco, and nor can it be used to describe the work of the city's Studio Choo, the floral team made up of best friends Jill Rizzo and Alethea Harampolis. Jill, who long resisted her family's florist roots in favor of becoming a "real artist," teamed up with Alethea in 2009; the duo honed their signature garden-in-a-vase style out of a kitchen, a Honda Element, and a garage before officially setting up shop a year later in South San Francisco. Seeking to echo the natural roadside beauty of their Bay Area surroundings, the two incorporate the rich variety of California's year-round greenery and branches into their wild arrangements, adding layers of fragrant rosemary, citrus-laden stems, and rambling vines of jasmine, passion flower, and hardenbergia. "We love anything that's juicy and full of life," Alethea says.

Jill and Alethea constantly keep an eye on their surrounding environment to discover unique color and texture combinations. "We're always looking for new ways to put together natural elements," says Jill. "Every stem's shape is unique and one bloom might fade faster than the next; twisting or turning of one element can completely change the look. Creating an arrangement is like the perfect combination of painting and sculpture." Studio Choo's regular workshops for aspiring and amateur florists reinforce the importance of perspective in floral practice for the designers themselves. "We try to remind our students that when laboring over an arrangement for a long time it can become hard to see. It is so important to take a moment to step back and notice the sections that have a particularly beautiful color blend or an interesting angle." Today, Jill and Alethea's perspective has widened to span both coasts. Jill now lives and works in Rhode Island, where she operates the studio's East Coast branch and partners with local farmers to design with the best of seasonal blooms, but the pair remains committed to working together on teaching, event, and garden design projects. "Studio Choo is a true collaboration based on a long friendship," says Alethea. "And we're always going to find a way to make that work."

A wreath crafted from foraged elements and ribbon dries gracefully.

"We love anything that's wild, rambling, and about to burst into bloom," Alethea says. "We like to think that our flowers look like a garden in a vase." FOLLOWING SPREAD: A late fall medley of amaryllises, dahlias, hellebores, and scabiosas includes foraged wild greens and berries.

FOLLOWING SPREAD: A Studio Choo installation of ranunculus, gardenias, orchids, hellebores, astilbes, and foraged and tropical greens spills out of a wooden structure in Honda, California.

Holly Vesecky + Rebecca Uchtman

HOLLYFLORA · LOS ANGELES, CALIFORNIA

A distinctly California vibe permeates all that emerges from Hollyflora, the Mid-City Los Angeles floral studio and boutique run by Holly Vesecky and Rebecca Uchtman. Friends and collaborators since 2003, the two met working at the West Hollywood flower shop The Velvet Garden. The pair "quickly took to each other's goofy sensibilities," and went into business together in 2006. Just as influenced by their state's scrubby chaparral landscapes and poppy fields as they are by the louche lifestyle of 1970s Laurel Canyon, Holly and Rebecca craft playful, wild arrangements that mix local native flowers—like proteas, banksias, and camellias—and favorites from all over the country, including lilacs, smokebushes, wild clematises, with treasures from the organic farm Holly's family owns in Ojai, California—blood oranges, succulents, and freshly picked herbs. "With the constant visual reference of social media, flowers can get muddled into a replica game," says Holly. "We try to step outside of that by drawing from abstract shapes, paint chips, and unusual blooms. We're constantly motivated by the work of artists like Paul Klee, Charlie Ray, and J. B. Blunk—and it's easy to be inspired when your partner is a weirdo!"

The resulting creations can be described as Dutch Masters meet the Mediterranean—lush, asymmetrical greenery; bold, brightly hued focal flowers; and trailing vines and branches, heavy with tropical citrus spilling out of textured ceramics, often handmade by Holly's husband, Josh Beckman. The foraged eclecticism that characterizes Hollyflora's floral styling carries over into the primarily California-crafted offerings in their boutique. Josh's pottery, textiles designed by close friend Heather Taylor, organic beauty products from Berkeley herbalists Earth Tu Face, beeswax candles hand-dipped by Holly, and a smattering of vintage ceramics and macramé all line the shelves of an airy 1920s warehouse infused with the coziness of a hand-built Big Sur cabin and the clean lines of a desert homestead. Outside lies a courtyard festooned with potted kumquat trees, bougainvillea, and draping passion flower and bleeding heart vines, all of which find their way into Hollyflora's arrangements. Says Holly, "We seek the beauty and wildness of nature with a sense of confidence and a wink."

Loquat branches and white proteas at Holly's family farm in Ojai, California.

ABOVE, RIGHT: A simple arrangement of wild grasses and fennel in a vase made by Holly's husband and frequent collaborator, Josh Beckman.

OPPOSITE: A Dutch Masters–inspired creation finds a home inside Hollyflora's shop.

FOLLOWING SPREAD: Holly cutting a branch of bougainvillea from Hollyflora's studio garden.

Sullivan Owen

PHILADELPHIA, PENNSYLVANIA

When Sullivan Owen sat down to plan her wedding in 2008, she was shocked to discover that none of the florists whom she and her husband-to-be met with were open to hearing her ideas about the decor for the event. Owen—then a retail merchandiser—had moonlighted in a flower shop as a teenager growing up in Manhattan, and understandably had strong and informed opinions about the design scheme of her wedding. This experience came as her "Aha!" moment, a realization that there existed a need for florists who appreciated a client's vision. In 2011, after a few years of apprenticing with local designers and taking classes at Flower School New York, Sullivan hung her own shingle with a studio in Philadelphia's Fishtown—and was named the best florist in the city by *Philadelphia* magazine a mere six months later.

Sullivan, an art-school dropout, uses asymmetrical shapes and complementary colors to create arrangements that evoke a sense of timelessness and nostalgia. Inspired by the legendary, colorful weekly flowers at the New York City restaurant La Grenouille, arranged by the eatery's owners, and the textural designs of French florist Christian Tortu, Sullivan embraces the bright and the bold, never one to shy away from unusual combinations like yellow and purple: "I like to make flowers that feel vibrant, fun, and alive." In addition to her knack for constructing large-scale branch installations, Sullivan also makes "little worlds," sprawling arrangements crafted out of flowers, mosses, and other natural materials, first as sets for stop-motion films and then as living art pieces for clients. "They're the most organic pieces I make, and it's a little bit like viewing a forest floor; I want people to imagine them to be whatever they can dream up, whether it be fairies or little creatures living within them." From these creations to her more structured floral work, Sullivan strives to use her talent to interpret her clients' visions: "My job is to convey emotion and help people celebrate life's most important moments through flowers. What could be more special than that?"

"My work is all about color and shape," Sullivan says. "I love vibrant, unexpected combinations."

Sullivan adds a Coral Charm peony as a bright finishing touch to one of her signature branch arrangements. **FOLLOWING SPREAD:** A "tiny world" made with organic materials—including lilies of the valley, ranunculus, and hellebores—sits atop a gnarled log.

"I'm all about controlled wildness," Sullivan says, balancing asymmetrical form with carefully considered composition.

Kristen Caissie

MOON CANYON · LOS ANGELES, CALIFORNIA

Los Angeles designer Kristen Caissie arranges dreamy florals in her Silver Lake flower studio, Moon Canyon, bringing to her organic creations a deeply cerebral background. "I began working with flowers at a shop in Boston while studying English literature in college," she says. "Using my hands was a welcome break from the norm; I loved being able to make something outside of thought." A New England native, she incorporates her early love for farmstand florals by tucking blooms with a freshly picked feel—daffodils in the spring, zinnias and clematises in the summer—into loose, leggy creations that spill out of their vessels. Kristen takes a poetic approach to her designs, using an earthy color palette and soft, textured flowers to craft wild, romantic arrangements.

The seasons—both the ferociously changing ones of her childhood and the more subtle variations of the Los Angeles climate—heavily influence Kristen's work. "I love watching how the landscape alters itself and how the different trees, grasses, and flora interact with one another: the textures of mixed wild grasses growing next to one another, how a passionvine takes over a palm tree, how bougainvillea grows up a redwood and shoots out and down some random limb." Kristen's literary roots and her artistic bent have long since cross-pollinated into a passion for flowers and an ease with the medium, apparent in the thoughtful placement of each and every stem in her designs. "Flowers are truly in my bones. It's the thing that speaks to me higher than all other forms of expression and in that is my freedom. I spent a large part of my younger days trying to get to know myself and flowers is it for me. The long hours, dirty hands, early flower market mornings, never really getting 'dressed for work,' wedding weekends—it all just fits. The work itself is what inspires and keeps me going."

A wild spirea arrangement spills out of a rocky Mojave Desert outcropping.

"With every season I fall in love with all the flowers all over again," Kristen says. "Every spring I cry over the daffodils, I love them so."

PREVIOUS SPREAD: Bright and cheerful roses and winter citrus. OPPOSITE: An arrangement with overflowing garden roses, foxgloves, ranunculus, and fritillarias sits above a serendipitously flowering beavertail cactus. ABOVE: Kristen installing in Pioneertown, California.

Kristen creating magic in her Los Angeles studio.
FOLLOWING SPREAD: Desert details.

Ashley Beyer

TINGE · SALT LAKE CITY, UTAH

When describing her relationship to her home state of Utah, Salt Lake City–based florist Ashley Beyer can't help but gush: "I remember driving up to Park City in the middle of spring as a teenager and looking out into the vastness of the canyons and my heart nearly stopping. You can drive an hour or two in any direction in Utah and be inspired by a completely different landscape, color palette, foliage, or plant—every bit of it is gorgeous." It's no surprise, then, that Ashley's stunning floral work—deeply influenced by her natural surroundings—can be similarly described as sumptuous layers of blooms with an emphasis on color and texture. Ashley, who worked in a flower shop throughout high school and college, spent many years in a cubicle before fully making the transition into floral design. "It was an emotional time because I spent so many years trying to find the right creative medium; as soon as I decided flowers were the path that I was meant to be on, it was as if they had been waiting for me all along."

Though Ashley credits Salt Lake City florist Sarah Winward, for whom she apprenticed on several weddings, with giving her a deep understanding of seamlessly executing large-scale events, she cites several of her fellow florists as influential to her work, particularly Nicolette Owen: "Her arrangements have a quiet, romantic beauty and effortless tranquility." Ashley's feminine, refined garden-inspired designs, rife with lush blossoms and trailing vines—honeysuckle is a favorite—emphasize subtle transitions in color and texture and seek to engender a sense of calm in the surrounding environment. For Ashley, her inner artist has certainly found her medium: "It's a constantly evolving art and you can push yourself creatively every time you begin a new arrangement. It's instant gratification, but just as quickly it's gone, which is what makes it exciting. The second you get that stem in your hand, the life left in it is short; you have to make it count!"

Ashley creates movement with gestural ranunculus, fritillaria, hellebore, tulips, and foraged branches.

Ashley arranging in her Salt Lake City studio. **FOLLOWING SPREAD:** Deconstructed spring elements, including ranunculus, muscaris, daffodils, Icelandic poppies, western chokecherries, and bleeding hearts.

"I draw a lot of inspiration from color themes I see in my surroundings, in art, or blooms themselves," Ashley says. "I'm constantly challenging myself to push new color palettes or find new ways to marry two unexpected colors together in pleasing ways."

Sarah Winward

HONEY OF A THOUSAND FLOWERS · SALT LAKE CITY, UTAH

The snowy peaks of the Rocky Mountains, Southern China's jagged, mystical karsts, the dusty sandstone and granite valleys of the Middle East, and England's overgrown thickets of rambling cabbage roses—these disparate landscapes inspire and shape the work of Sarah Winward, a lifelong traveler and Utah-based floral designer. Picking wildflowers for bouquets on walks through her Salt Lake City neighborhood rapidly evolved into a bustling career for Sarah and she started her business, Honey of a Thousand Flowers. The name is a nod to the variety of nectars from which her backyard hive of bees drink, and it speaks neatly to the plethora of global influences and materials that comprise her abundant, wild arrangements. Says Sarah, "My flowers are a product of everything that is around me, quite literally."

As she travels the globe for a handful of far-flung weddings every year, each new location pushes Sarah to creatively reflect and utilize her surroundings. She constructs intricate floral dreamscapes brimming with seasonally appropriate blooms—delicate spring blossoms like gestural fritillarias, showy magnolias, and fragrant lilacs are among her favorites—and masses of textural foliage hand-culled from the event's site. Serving primarily as a destination florist not only indulges her passion for exploration but also forces her to keep her work fresh, perennially creating site-specific designs—arches dripping with branches and flowers, altars encircled by arrangements crafted from tall grasses, canopies of greens over the dining tables—and never repeating a combination of colors or textures. Sarah, who studied under powerhouses like Ariella Chezar and at Brooklyn's Little Flower School with Sarah Ryhanen and Nicolette Owen, has in turn passed her romantic style on to a new generation of florists in and around Salt Lake City, including Ashley Beyer of Tinge and Nicole Land of Soil and Stem. And when her own well of inspiration needs refilling, it's time for her to simply hit the road again: "When I'm traveling I can focus on all of the simple things that make me love life, which refreshes me and makes me want to create. I have such a great respect for the earth, and that's what brings me to love flowers so much."

An installation of pear branches against the backdrop of Salt Lake City's snowy spring canyons.

FOLLOWING SPREAD: Sarah layers in the best of spring's flowers—several varieties of fritillaria, as well as lilacs, pear blossoms, hellebores, and bleeding hearts.

"I'm drawn to the wildness of nature," Sarah says. "I hope that my flowers evoke the same wild feelings in others when they're viewing them as they do to me when I'm creating them." **FOLLOWING SPREAD:** Ikebana-style blossoms foraged from Sarah's backyard against an onyx backdrop.

Holly Carlisle

ROSEGOLDEN FLOWERS · BIRMINGHAM, ALABAMA

For Holly Carlisle, a florist and photographer in Birmingham, Alabama flowers do more than just beautify a room, provide sympathy, or express thanks—they have the power to redirect the trajectory of an entire life. A former makeup artist and hairstylist, Holly was so captivated by the peonies that she bought to decorate the tables at her post-elopement reception that she was inspired to transition into floral design: "A good peony can alter your whole existence!" An art-school background armed her with a carefully trained eye for composition and a newfound zeal for flowers with a passion that makes room for the blossoms to speak for themselves. Holly, who has studied and worked with Sarah Ryhanen of Saipua, has an aesthetic that is at once both evocative and controlled, striking a meticulous balance between overgrown and manicured. "I would say that 50 percent of my working relationship with flowers is expressive and process-driven and the other half is quite studied and pensive."

Though she cites abstract expressionists like Robert Rauschenberg and Cy Twombly as influential to her work (which is apparent in her thoughtfully mixed color palette), Holly also pays homage to the grande dame of Southern interiors, Dorothy Draper, in her cheerful, bold floral choices—ripe, heavy-petaled ranunculus, voluptuous Coral Charm peonies, amaryllises. "I love the softness and gentility of the South and know that as a native of the region, it finds its way into my work whether my more rebellious side likes it or not," Holly says. At its heart, her work is about paying a deep, abiding respect to the blooms that changed the course of her life and career. "I feel like it's my responsibility to reveal flowers at the most beautiful point in their lifespan, which usually happens to be the most open and fragile."

Holly's maximalist take on Ikebana.

FOLLOWING SPREAD: A fresh, white arrangement crafted from entirely foraged elements, including azaleas, dogwoods, and spireas.

"I believe in finding the right flower for each moment in each arrangement," Holly says. "Not just the right variety of flower, but the right flower in that particular instance in place and time." FOLLOWING SPREAD: Specimens from Holly's foraged arrangement.

Nicole Land

SOIL AND STEM · HOLLADAY, UTAH

Throughout the various stages of her life, Nicole Land has maintained a deep connection with the natural world, from picking and pressing wildflowers as a child, hiking through canyons with her husband, and, most recently, tending to a flock of hens and a honeybee hive with her toddler daughter on their small plot of land just outside Salt Lake City. After being tapped to do the flowers for her little sister's wedding, Nicole discovered a passion for floral design, first learning the basics at a small local shop, then with Sarah Winward, fellow Utah florist and owner of Honey of a Thousand Flowers. "My first designer crush was Ariella Chezar, but Sarah really opened my eyes to the reasons why we put flowers in certain places; she helped me to understand the importance of depth, layering, and seeing my work as creating art through a floral medium."

Out of her studio in the Wasatch Mountains come feminine, romantic arrangements crafted from flowers that Nicole tries to source locally as much as possible. "I feel these stems have character that mass-produced greenhouse flowers do not. They reflect life in a way that is really beautiful to me—some are weathered and imperfect, while others, newly bloomed, are pure loveliness." There is a graceful softness to her work that is largely predicated on the raw elements with which she composes her creations: outdoor-grown, heirloom roses with their layers of plush petals; airy, delicate sweet peas; and lately, arching stems of delicate, bell-shaped campanulas. Nicole, who intends for her arrangements to look as if they're continuing to grow from the garden, strives to build an effortless narrative with her florals: "The stems I use tell stories, and when paired together, they create a novel of beginnings, middles, and endings. Some flowers are the heroines while others are supporting characters; collectively, they create a piece of art that holds interest, dimension, and emotion." Her inspiration from the natural world may have evolved since she was a child, but it continues to serve as the foundation for her florals: "The authentic connection to the earth that I feel when I'm collecting fruit from our small orchard with my daughter or cutting flowers from our yard allows me to produce work that remains true to the beauty of nature."

Nicole plays with negative space and evokes the Dutch Masters with a combination of hellebore, flowering spring branches, and foraged twigs.

Nicole with an armful of plum branches.

THIS SPREAD: A bountiful arrangement of garden roses and ornamental plum branches. "I'm a sucker for heritage garden roses for their full-faced look and layers of plush petals," Nicole says. "They perfectly reflect my spirited, natural, and fresh aesthetic." FOLLOWING SPREAD: A massing of crabapple and viburnum blossoms amidst a still-barren spring landscape.

Acknowledgments

There's so much to be thankful for. First, thanks to Ken Miller, who came up with the good idea (and title!) for this book. Thank you to each of the incredible floral designers, who contributed significant amounts of time and resources to create the arrangements we photographed (especially Taylor Patterson, our confidant, advisor, and flower muse throughout); to Lindsey Taylor, the amazing floral designer, writer, collaborator, and an early supporter of our work in flowers; to Charles Miers, our publisher at Rizzoli, for having the foresight to make this book happen; to our editor at Rizzoli, Julie Schumacher Grubbs, for the minutia of countless emails and conversations as the book took shape, and especially for completely trusting us with our vision and letting us see it through; to Martynka Wawrzyniak, for gracefully picking up the editing from the layout stage through to print; to Su Barber, best friend and the very best designer we could hope for to give shape to the pages and our photography; to Stella Bugbee, for the book's introduction and for constant inspiration; to Katie Henry, for powering through the chapter intro texts and a pregnancy simultaneously; to our sweet children, Oliver and Isabel, for letting us cart them around endlessly on shoot after shoot and for picking us the most beautiful bouquets; and thank you to all those who took care of them along the way, especially Grannie Jane, Auntie Gurumaan, and "YaYa." And, finally, thank you to our parents, for creating the gardens that instilled the love of flowers in us.